TEAM-BUILDING

TEAM-BUILDING: FROM THE BENCH TO THE BOARDROOM

Pat Sullivan

*This book is dedicated to my college coach, mentor,
dear friend, and the best Team Builder I have ever known
– Gordie Gillespie.*

TABLE OF CONTENTS

AUTHORS' QUOTES

"A fantastic book based on the wisdom of one of the most highly-revered and respected men who ever coached high school and college sports...Brief, remarkable lessons that translate from sports to business. More than that though, these are lessons for living a joyous, happy, abundant, and fulfilling life."

Bob Burg, co-author of The Go-Giver and
The Go-Giver Influencer

"Pat Sullivan modeled 'Team-Building' every day in the classroom, the gymnasium, and in the board room at the University of St. Francis. He was not only a great leader, but the perfect mentor for all of us who played and coached for him. There are not enough superlatives to describe his character and wisdom. Enjoy this book as you will see just how extraordinary Coach Sullivan is as a 'Team-Builder.'"

Randy Stelter, co-author of
A Teacher's Guide to The Go-Giver

"Anything Pat Sullivan writes is worth the time for leaders, teachers, coaches, and parents. He already hit a home run with his first book, Attitude-The Cornerstone of Leadership; this book is another 'miss-your-subway-stop' read."

Tom Anstett, author of Stop Whining; Start Winning [for teachers and coaches}

"As an educator for 43 years, a former basketball coach, and an independent business owner, I have read countless books on team-building and leadership. None are better than Pat Sullivan's recent book on Team-Building. What struck me about this book was that Pat takes the best principles from noteworthy individuals from both coaching and the business community and weaves them into an understandable and easy to adapt framework. Every organizational leader should read this book. I plan to buy multiple copies and give them to friends who lead churches, teams, and businesses. You should do the same."

Frank Palmasani, author of Right College, Right Price

"Pat Sullivan is one of the best coaches I have ever known, and I have known a lot of coaches. He laid the foundation for the basketball program at Providence and did the same at the University of St. Francis.

...In recent years I have spoken with Pat at various businesses. His message on Attitude, Leadership, and Team-Building definitely resonates with audiences.

Rudy Ruettiger, from the movie "RUDY"

FOREWORD

I have known Pat Sullivan since he taught and coached at Providence Catholic High School in the 1960s and '70s, but our roots extend deeper than that—we both grew up in the old steel town of Joliet, Illinois, and we both attended Joliet Catholic High School. I would rank him among the best coaches I have ever known, and I have known a lot of coaches. He laid the foundation for the basketball program at Providence and did the same at the University of St. Francis.

Pat always saw beyond the narrow confines of a basketball court. He cared about the success of his players off the court, and he stressed the importance of earning their degrees; remarkably, 98 percent of the seniors who played for him at St. Francis have their degrees today. Equally, if not more importantly, he wanted them to be young men of character. Given the success of so many of his former players in their careers, I'd say he accomplished both of these goals. In addition to these primary goals, his teams at Providence and St. Francis won 602 games.

In recent years, I have spoken with Pat at various businesses and organizations. His message on attitude, leadership, and team-building definitely resonates with audiences. He has been inducted into eight Halls of Fame, he has been named coach of the year more times than I can count, and he has received a number of lifetime achievement awards. Upon his retirement, the University of St. Francis renamed their recreation center the Pat Sullivan Center.

The twenty concepts presented in the book will help leaders build their teams. As someone who walked on to the football team at the University of Notre Dame and who has sat in many boardrooms, I wholeheartedly agree with Pat that the concepts used in building a team in athletics are no different from the concepts used in building a team in business. This book will give the readers the opportunity to reflect, as Pat writes, "on their philosophies and policies of team-building."

I hope you enjoy this insightful read from my friend, Pat Sullivan, and that it enhances your team-building skills.

Sincerely,
Rudy Ruettiger
The movie *Rudy*

PREFACE

We played the University of San Francisco on December 27, 1994. They were better than we were at every position. They had two 7 footers, a 6'8" power forward, two jet-quick guards, and the last pick of the first round in the 1995 NBA draft. They also had tradition. The great Bill Russell's, K. C. Jones's, and Bill Cartwright's numbers hung on the wall, and in our locker room, they had pictures of twenty-two former players who put on NBA jerseys. We were the team and university few people had heard of. Our former players attended NBA games, but no one had put on a jersey!

Despite the above disadvantages, we were a good TEAM, and we did beat them that night, 81-80.

In the following pages, I would like to share some concepts that I believe are important in athletic team-building. These concepts come from the **BENCH.** I have forty-four years of experience in building basketball teams—ten years at the high school level and thirty-four at the collegiate level. I also have thirty-four years of developing a collegiate athletic department, serving 370 student athletes and sixty coaches. I believe the concepts that I identify in team-building in athletics are no different from team-building in the business world. In each chapter I will first address a concept that can be important in building a team in athletics. I will then follow the athletic concept with research I have done about that concept in the business arena. That research will be to the **BOARDROOM**.

In Red Auerbach's book, *Let Me Tell You a Story*, the famed Boston Celtics coach met with buddies in his retirement years for regular breakfasts. At these get-togethers, he would entertain his friends with his many stories from the Celtics lore, beginning the conversation always with the phrase "Let me tell you a story." Like Red, I have used many stories to emphasize the twenty concepts in team-building in the athletic arena.

I sincerely hope you enjoy the read.

Pat Sullivan

CHAPTER 1
CARING

A favorite quotation of the late Rick Majerus, former University of Utah and St. Louis University basketball coach, was John Maxwell's "Nobody cares how much you know until they know how much you care."

Leaders who are great team builders care about the people in their charge far beyond the narrow confines of a basketball court, a football field, or a workplace.

Coaches must demand that their players play hard every night in practice, both mentally and physically. They have to be tough and demanding on their athletes because the games are tough. Winning is tough.

When I watched Rick Majerus's teams practice at both Utah and St. Louis, he was very demanding. He accepted nothing but the players' best efforts throughout the practice, and when they weren't giving it, he let them know in no uncertain terms.

I can remember the first time my children, when they were very young, saw me at a practice. When we got home, they told me they had never seen me act like that before. I was very vocal in demanding hard work because I always believed in legendary former UCLA coach John Wooden's maxim "There is no substitute for hard work." Practice is the venue where teams learn the habit of competing with maximum effort.

Why can coaches push players so hard?

I believe there is one main answer to this question. The players know how much the coaches care about them, on and off the court or field. When the players know how much the coaches care when they are playing for them and will continue to care about their welfare when they are no longer playing for them, they will accept the coaches' demands.

We were very fortunate to have a player transfer to us right before school started in my first year at the College—now the University—of St. Francis. He was a football player who had received an NCAA scholarship to a Division I school. He went to that school with a high school teammate. His high school friend suffered a concussion during the first week of practice and was hospitalized for a few days. During his stay in the hospital, not one coach from the football staff visited him. Our transfer did not want to play for coaches who didn't care about their athletes, so he called us about coming to St. Francis and playing basketball, a sport he had also played in high school. He played four years at

St. Francis and went on to have a very successful career in the business field.

The NBA's San Antonio Spurs coach, Greg Popovich, showed that he cared. Our players demonstrated at a Nike clinic that had only NBA coaches as presenters. We had to demonstrate Friday evening and all day Saturday. Popovich was the last presenter on Saturday, coming on at 8:00 p.m. Needless to say, our players were quite tired, and one of them, Arvydas Astrauskas, had turned his ankle badly while demonstrating a drill.

Two weeks after the clinic, we received a call from Coach Popovich. He asked for the injured player's name and number so he could call him. Arvydas was so surprised that a famous NBA coach would take the time to call him that he thought it was a prank call! Coach didn't stop there. He invited our entire team to be his guests at his game against the Chicago Bulls. After the game, he came to us and shook hands with every player. I am sure Coach Popovich had never heard of St. Francis prior to the clinic, but he did care about our injured player and his teammates. No wonder why NBA players respect him so much.

Bob Knight, the Indiana University and Texas Tech coach, also showed he cared. Our players demonstrated for him at a Chicago-area high school where he presented for six hours. There were eight hundred coaches at the clinic, and there was no question that our guys had to be nervous presenting for Coach Knight in front of all those coaches. They got confused on the very first drill Coach asked them to demonstrate. The coaches laughed. Coach Knight then went to the center of the bleachers and told all eight hundred coaches that our kids had made the sacrifice of leaving campus at 6:00 a.m. and that they were there to help him teach. He went on to tell the coaches if he heard any more laughing, he was going to pick ten of them to demonstrate, and our players would sit in the front row and laugh at them. You could not believe how quiet eight hundred coaches could become! You could also immediately see how much our guys appreciated Coach Knight's caring about them.

Caring does build strong, loyal teams.

From the Boardroom
Oprah Winfrey showed she cared for her employees in three different ways:

- She wanted everyone in her organization, regardless of position or title, treated with dignity. In her article "What It's Really Like to Work for Oprah," Emily Co wrote, "From the janitors to the high-ranking executives, Oprah demands that everyone should be treated equally, with the same amount of respect."
- Great leaders make it a practice to know their people by name. Janet Lee, senior field producer

for *The Oprah Winfrey Show*, affirmed that Oprah did this in the article "What's It Like to Have Oprah for a Boss." Lee wrote, "What was amazing with her was that the company grew and grew every year and we had more people and departments and she remembered everyone's name. I always thought that was amazing."

- Oprah stood up for her female employees early in her career. This stand was substantiated in the article "Oprah Winfrey Fought for Her Female Employees to Get Equal Pay." Oprah stated in this article, "I was making a lot of money and my producers were being paid poorly. I went to my boss at the time and said 'everybody needs a raise' and he said 'they're only girls. They're a bunch of girls. What do they need more money for?' I go 'well either they're going to get raises or I'm gonna sit down. I will not work unless they get paid.' And they did."

Indra Nooyi, chairman and CEO of PepsiCo, validated that she cared for her employees beyond the workplace in the article "Why Microsoft and Everyone Else Loves the Indian CEO." Nooyi stated, "You need to look at the employees and say, 'I value you as a person. I know you have a life beyond PepsiCo and I'm going to respect you for your entire life, not just treat you as employee number 4,567.'"

Caring does lead to success in both the athletic arena and the business world. Oprah Winfrey and Indra Nooyi are extraordinarily successful business leaders who care about the people they are leading.

CHAPTER 2
KNOWLEDGE

Knowledge generates respect.

If you are to build a team, you must have knowledge of the organization you are trying to build. Whether it's a business, an athletic team, or a church, if you do not have expertise in the venture you are trying to build, why should people follow you? You don't have to be a genius, but you have to know your field.

When I reflect on coaches who I felt really knew basketball, three names immediately come to mind—Rick Majerus; Hubie Brown, a two-time NBA coach of the year; and Bob Knight.

I was fortunate to work with Rick in week-long overnight summer camps. The greatest number of week-long camps I worked in one summer was five, two of them back to back. I was exhausted after these five camps. Rick often worked twelve straight weeks of camps! His head coach at the time, Marquette's Al McGuire, could get Rick into most of the camps in the country. So Rick would go from John Wooden's camp in Los Angeles to North Carolina with Dean Smith, the famed University of North Carolina coach, to Bob Knight's camp in Indiana. In between those camps, he would work with us in the Medalist Sports Education camps.

His work with these great coaches increased his basketball knowledge exponentially. He became one of the most knowledgeable coaches I have ever known. When I watched his practices at both Utah and St. Louis, the respect his players had for him was obvious. When Rick taught, everyone listened.

We were also very fortunate to have Hubie Brown speak at our Medalist camps three times each summer. Every time he presented, we all learned something about the game we had never thought of! His knowledge was and is truly amazing.

When he was an assistant at Duke University, Hubie, like Rick, worked camps up and down the East Coast. By the time he became the head coach of the NBA Atlanta Hawks, he had superb knowledge of the game. When my good friend and fellow coach, the late Bill Gleason, and I visited Hubie's preseason camp in Atlanta, the respect his players had for his teaching was very evident. One of his players, who had played on five NBA teams prior to coming to Atlanta, told Bill and me that he learned more basketball from Hubie than the other five coaches combined! Hubie continues to share his basketball knowledge with us today as an NBA television analyst.

Bob Knight may have had more respect for older coaches than any coach I have ever met. He always made time to learn from them, and when he became famous, he constantly honored them. When he developed his motion offense, he did it with the great Pete Newell, a coach whose teams won the NCAA, the NIT, and the Olympics. He also had Coach Newell present with him when he did his One-Man Clinics. I think Coach Knight would attribute much of his immense knowledge of the game to the many older coaches he knew, worked with, and learned from.

It is no surprise that the above three coaches were in demand to speak at clinics throughout our country and internationally. Their great basketball knowledge earned them respect from coaches all over the world.

Knowledge leads to respect, and respect leads to building great teams.

From the Boardroom
Adele Helsall spoke strongly to the importance of knowledge in the business world in Digitalist when she wrote the following: "Demonstrating strong knowledge and expertise of your product is crucial for creating a positive customer experience and instilling faith and trust within the customer. Without accurate or

available product knowledge your products may as well be worthless."

"Understanding the Importance of Product Knowledge in B2B Sales" was published in *tenfold*. It emphasizes how critical knowledge is in the business world. "Product knowledge is essential for any sales organization. To foster positive customer experiences and create trust between reps and prospects, showing strong expertise of your solutions is crucial...Having a deep understanding of your product allows reps to tell prospects how your solution will make a difference in their operations, whether it's going to make their operations more efficient, their employees more productive, or their pipeline fuller and more active."

In her outstanding blog, Product Knowledge Training, Brenda Fernandez states four reasons why product knowledge is so essential:

Product knowledge is the most important tool for closing sales. It instills faith, trust, and respect in the customer.

The benefits of product knowledge are as follows:

- Strengthens Communication Skills—A thorough and wider understanding of a product enables a salesperson to use different techniques and methods of presenting a product to various types of customers.

- Boosts Enthusiasm—A deep product knowledge, a display of enthusiasm, and belief in the product may generate excitement among your customers and alleviate uncertainty about the solution that the product provides for the customer.
- Grows Confidence—If a customer isn't fully committed to completing a sale, the difference may simply be the presence (or lack) of credibility or confidence a salesperson has toward the product. Becoming educated in the product and its uses will help cement that confidence.
- Assists in Overcoming Objectives—Factual information gained from product knowledge may be used to strike down objections. Solid knowledge about your product coupled with parallel information about similar products sold by your competitors gives you that added advantage to easily counter objections.

Rick Majerus, Hubie Brown, and Bob Knight would have been excellent in sales because they surely knew their product!

CHAPTER 3

CONTINUOUS LEARNING

Continuous learning leads to wisdom. Leaders with wisdom can build great teams.

John Wooden's UCLA basketball teams won ten NCAA national championships in the last twelve years he coached. His teams also won seven of these championships in a row. I don't think either record will ever be eclipsed. A friend, Pete Turgovich, played on Coach Wooden's last team. With all the success Coach had *and* at the age of sixty-five, he told Pete and his teammates how much he was still learning about the game. John Wooden was a lifelong learner.

Gordie Gillespie accomplished what I don't believe will ever happen again. He was a head football coach in high school and a head baseball, basketball, and football coach at the collegiate level. His teams won an incredible 2,402 games! He is the second-winningest coach in the history of college baseball. I played four years of college baseball for Gord. Three years after I graduated, he asked me to come back to work a baseball camp with him. I thought I knew his teaching because I was only three years removed from playing for him. It was a real surprise for me to see how much Gordie's teaching had advanced in such a short time span. Gordie coached college baseball until the age of eighty-five and never stopped learning!

I was extremely fortunate to have many outstanding assistant coaches in my years at St. Francis, but two stood out. I had John Cornelius for my first thirteen years and Jack Hermanski for my last twenty-four years. Both were great men and superb coaches. Jack had an interesting point about our continuous learning when it came to basketball drills. He said that in our first decade of coaching, we used many drills. We may not have known the purpose of a drill, but we used it simply because it was a good drill. In the second decade, we eliminated some of the drills. In the third decade and beyond, we had very few drills and hoped the ones we kept were game pragmatic. The evolution of our teaching led to drilling only situations that our players would experience in games.

The same thing happened in our weight training program. We obviously lifted for strength. However, after a five-hour session with the Chicago Bulls strength coaches, we changed our approach. They taught us to lift for athleticism, not just strength. We then advanced our program to lift for both strength and quickness. We experienced continuous learning because we were fortunate to find people who were teaching better than we were.

As I came into my last years of coaching, I made another change to better my learning. I identified coaches whom I greatly respected and scheduled one-on-one meetings with them. I found these sessions to be very insightful and productive learning situations.

I once heard someone say the mind is like a parachute; it works best when it's open.

Great team builders keep an open mind and never stop learning.

From the Boardroom
Henry Ford had this interesting observation on continuous learning: "Anyone who stops learning is old, whether at twenty or eighty. Anyone who keeps learning stays young."

Davis Tucker had this to say in *The 60 Second Marketer*: "When it comes to running a business, knowledge is power. You need to know so much about so many different aspects, sometimes it can be a bit overwhelming. But the great thing about business is you're constantly learning. If not, your business won't be evolving...You need to be constantly learning what move to make next in order to be successful."

Ursula Burns, chairman and CEO of Xerox Corporation, gave this advice to MIT graduates in her commencement address: "I hope none of you will think of your diploma as an end-point. This event is called a commencement, not a curtain-call. You've been given a wonderful academic foundation—an invitation to begin a journey of lifelong learning. No less an authority than Albert Einstein wrote that, 'Learning is not a product of schooling but the lifelong attempt to acquire it.'"

Michael Simmons wrote an article in *Quartz* titled "Be like Bill Gates and Warren Buffett: If You're Not Spending 5 Hours per Week Learning, You're Being Irresponsible." He wrote that Buffett "has invested 80% of his time reading and thinking throughout his career" and that Gates reads a book a week and "has taken a yearly two week reading vacation throughout his career."

Simmons summed up continuous learning when he wrote, "Learning is the single best investment of our time that we can make. Or as Benjamin Franklin said, 'An investment in knowledge pays the best interest.'"

John Wooden at sixty-five and Gordie Gillespie at eighty-five would have been successful businessmen because they never stopped learning.

CHAPTER 4
FAILURE

In the last ten to fifteen years, there has been a change in American youth sports. We don't want our young people to experience failure in contests, so we give everyone a trophy. I believe that by doing this, we are failing to educate our youth. Failure is a part—in fact, a big part—of life. Most, if not all, of us will meet failure personally and/or professionally. There is a lot of adversity out there, and none of us are exempt. Rather than giving everyone a trophy, I believe we would better serve our young people by allowing them to fail and teaching them how to deal with it.

I was working in Salt Lake City, Utah, when I heard former LSU Coach Dale Brown say your FQ was more important than your IQ. I had no idea what he meant until he told us your FQ is your failure quotient—how often can you fail and have the resiliency to get back up? Getting up after failing is one of the most important lessons of life.

Thomas Edison is said to have failed ten thousand times in his experiments to find electricity. When his friends asked him why he kept trying after so many failures, he told them because now he knew ten thousand ways it would not work! He definitely had a strong FQ.

When you read about Abraham Lincoln's political journey to the presidency, you find many more failures than successes. His norm was not to win elections but to lose them. His failures, therefore, were very public. However, he had the resiliency to keep going and ultimately became one of the best presidents, if not the best, in United States history.

When his teacher flunked him in sixth grade, he wrote that this student was "dumb and hopeless." Thank God Winston Churchill had a strong FQ, as he went on to become perhaps the greatest leader of the twentieth century.

Dan Ruettiger, of the movie *Rudy* fame, tells audiences in his many speaking engagements throughout the country that he graduated third in his high school class...that is, third from the bottom. When he told people in our city, Joliet, Illinois, that he was going to Notre Dame, he was laughed at. When he went on to say that at 5'9" and 185 pounds he was going to play football there, the laughter grew louder. Rudy accomplished both goals, and the two themes in his presentations today are never give up and never let anyone tell you you're too dumb to accomplish your goals.

My brother, Dan, is a good friend of Rudy's. At the beginning of his senior year at Providence Catholic High School, the principal called him in and asked how he could possibly rank ninety-ninth of 106. Dan told him because he never wanted to get into the triple figures! Dan went on to become an excellent classroom teacher, an outstanding high school coach in football, basketball, and baseball, and is finishing his career as a principal. He has helped thousands of kids along the way, especially that kid in the back of the room who doesn't care to study, because he has been that kid.

The field of cybernetics tells us there are two ways to deal with failure:

- Learn from it.
- Put it behind you.

The people cited above did both—even though they didn't get a trophy.

Most great accomplishments have failure in their backgrounds, but their leaders had strong FQs and led them through the failure.

From the Boardroom
Warren Buffett is the third-richest man in the world, but he sure knew failure along the way. In fact, at one

point in his life, he said this of his extraordinarily successful company: "I would have been better off if I'd never heard of Berkshire Hathaway."

In "Warren Buffett: Profile in Failure," he had this insight on failure: "The greatest people in history have been failures. Certainly, we remember these people as successes—success stories—and we treat those stories as legends and those individuals as gods. But each of them failed epically and repeatedly, more so than the combined successes of all humanity...Failure should not be overlooked in anyone, especially not those we admire. It is through failure that these individuals were able to learn, grow, and ultimately succeed...The most successful people in the world have had an abundance of failure."

Arianna Huffington, cofounder and editor in chief of Huffington Post, in an interview with Issie Lapowsky said, "My mother used to call failure a stepping-stone to success. When you frame failure that way, it changes dramatically what you're willing to do, how you're willing to invent, and the risks you'll take."

When she failed in her 2003 run for governor of California, she wrote how she accepted her mother's advice when she stated, "I also learned about myself, about communicating, being able to touch people's hearts and minds, and listening. All the things that were ingrained in me during the campaign definitely had an impact in forming Huffington Post."

Kevin O'Leary, a *Shark Tank* investor and founder of O'Leary Funds, took failure to another level when he wrote, "I like to invest in entrepreneurs who have failed at least once. And they have the sting of failure in their DNA. Because then they know how important it is to have a business plan and to execute it."

Athletes can make solid business people because they meet failure regularly. A baseball player is a good hitter when he fails seven of ten at-bats. A good three-point shooter in basketball fails on six out of every ten shots. A quality soccer player can fail to score in a number of consecutive games. But each of them learns from his or her failures and moves on.

CHAPTER 5
SUCCESS

Success is often the product of failure.

Winston Churchill said it this way: "Success is going from failure to failure without losing enthusiasm."

Pat Riley, the former Los Angeles Laker coach and current Miami Heat president, said, "Success is getting up one more time than you have been knocked down."

Vince Lombardi, the legendary Green Bay Packer coach, said, "The glory in sport is not in never falling but it's in getting up after the fall."

And only Yogi Berra, the great Yankee catcher, could see it this way, "90% of success is mental; the other 50% is physical."

I have always believed that success and failure go hand in hand. Most achievements have known failure.

I taught and coached at Providence High School in New Lenox, Illinois, for ten wonderful years. I thought we were developing an outstanding school. We had quality leadership, a dedicated faculty, and really great students. However, the Joliet Diocesan School Board felt differently. They studied the ten schools in the diocese and elected to close Providence in 1968 due to financial problems. Administrators, faculty, students, and parents banded together and petitioned the bishop to keep the school open. Bishop Romeo Blanchette, to his great credit, had the courage to veto his own committee, which had put a year's study into its decision. Providence certainly has had failure in its background, but today it is one of the best schools in the diocese from an academic, athletic, and extracurricular activities perspective.

Tom Dedin was the Providence athletic director and soccer, basketball, and baseball coach when I arrived there in 1965. We had an athletic program for only three years, and we definitely knew failure. As Tom and I used to reflect, it was not whether we could win a basketball game; it was whether we could get the ball across the midcourt line! Due to Tom's leadership, Providence gradually became an outstanding athletic program. From initial failure, Providence has now won an incredible thirty state championships in all of its sports.

Two additional thoughts on success.

My favorite insight on success was written by that person who wrote so many erudite, meaningful quotes,

Mr. Anonymous: "Success is never owned; it's only rented and the rent is due every day." You never have it made.

The minute you think you have it made, the minute you think you have arrived, the minute you think you can coast in athletics, you are in trouble. The games I hated to coach the most were the ones where we had more talent than the opponents. Our players knew we were more talented, and no matter what we said as coaches, they often felt the game was over when we stepped on the floor. All we had to do was show up. They forgot the rent was due every day.

I have no way of knowing, but I have to believe that a major part of our beating Goliath, the University of San Francisco, was the above attitude. They were unquestionably more talented than we were at every position, and I am sure they didn't take us seriously. But success is never owned.

Secondly, success can lead to arrogance. I find it interesting that most of the people, regardless of profession, who have made it to the top of their profession are humble. However, the people on the rise, the ones who have not quite made it, seem to be the arrogant ones. They have all the answers, and you have none. It may benefit them and everyone on the road to success to reflect on this from Coach Wooden:

Talent is God given, so be humble.
Fame is man given, so be grateful.

But conceit is self-given and you better be careful.

Humility is not a bad virtue for leaders and team builders to strive for.

From the Boardroom

Dale Carnegie wrote often about failure leading to success. In "Top Quotes from Dale Carnegie on Secrets of Mega Success," he stated it this way:

- "Most of the important things in the world have been accomplished by people who kept on trying where there seemed to be no hope at all."
- "Develop success from failure. Discouragement and failure are two of the surest stepping stones to success."

Henry Ford, in "38 Memorable Henry Ford Quotes," addressed how important it is to stay humble when successful:

- "I believe God is managing affairs and that He doesn't need any advice from me."
- "As we advance in life we learn the limits of our abilities."

Ford also emphasized the importance of teamwork in successful ventures when he wrote, "Coming together is a beginning; keeping together is progress; working together is success."

Barbara Corcoran, a *Shark Tank* investor, in "10 Inspiration Quotes from Women Business Leaders," had a very blunt comment about successful people and those who don't succeed when she wrote, "The difference between successful people and others is how long they spend time feeling sorry for themselves."

Melinda Gates, cofounder of the Bill and Melinda Gates Foundation, took success to another level when she wrote, "If you are successful, it is because somewhere, sometime, someone gave you a life or an idea that started you in the right direction. Remember also that you are indebted to life until you help some less fortunate person, just as you were helped."

Instead of success leading to arrogance, it surely seems better to reach down and help others to attain their successes, both in the athletic and the business venues.

CHAPTER 6
HUMOR

Humor can play a big part in team-building.
Every coach has to push his team to work. He has to demand hard work every day in practice. There is no question about that, but fun and humor can and should be interspersed with the work.

Rick Majerus gave us a drill that was fun for our players. We often used it at the end of practice so we could all leave on a good note. The drill was called "Utes (Utah) Win." We divided our players into two teams—our big guys at one end of the court and our perimeter players at the other end. Each team had two balls. The shooters started at the elbows, shot in single file, and when they made five baskets, they went to the other end of the court and once again had to make five baskets from the elbows. When each team made the ten required baskets, they went to the midcourt line, where they shot at opposite baskets. The first team to make the half-court shot was the winner. The guys would be cheering for their teammates, and the balls would be flying all over the gym. Finally, one ball would go in, and that team would have quite a celebration! The players truly enjoyed "Saints Win," the new name we gave to Rick's drill. It was a lot of fun.

Vince Lombardi was the epitome of a tough coach. In his book *Instant Replay*, Jerry Kramer, a player on the great Green Bay Packers teams of the sixties, writes that Lombardi once fined Paul Hornung and Max McGee for missing curfew. He then told them that if they missed curfew again, the fine would be substantially higher. After thinking about the potential exorbitant fine, Lombardi told them that wherever they would be going for that fine, he'd like to go with them. Lombardi could lighten the mood.

Our St. Francis football team, coached by Gordie Gillespie, used to practice at a park right next to a cemetery. Dan Sharp, our offensive coordinator, enjoyed telling this story about Gord. Our offense was running through timing plays with no defense. They totally messed up a certain play. Gordie said nothing. They ran it wrong a second time, and again Gord said nothing. After the third miscue, Gordie went over to the fence separating the field from the graveyard. The players were simply standing and watching as Gordie faced the graves, cupped his hands, and yelled at the graves,

"Hey, fellas...hey, fellas, make room for Gordie. These guys are killing me!"

Our dear friend, the late Kevin Donlan, was refereeing a Marquette–Notre Dame game in Milwaukee. Al McGuire was the Marquette coach and Digger Phelps the Notre Dame coach. Kevin went to administer a free throw, and none other than Coach McGuire was at the free-throw line telling Kevin what a lousy call he had just made. Kevin told Al that for every step he had to take to get back to the bench, he was going to assess one technical foul. Al thought for a second, then called for two of his players, put his arms around their shoulders, and had them carry him back to the bench. Kevin made the decision: no steps, no technicals—much to the chagrin of Coach Phelps.

In all businesses and athletics, there is a great deal of pressure to win, to be successful. Humor and fun can and do dissipate pressure.

From the Boardroom

Allison Beard had these insights on the importance of humor in the business world in her article "Leading with Humor" in the *Harvard Business Review*: "The workplace needs laughter. According to institutions as serious as Wharton, MIT, and London Business School, every chuckle or guffaw brings with it a host of business benefits. Laughter relieves stress and boredom, boosts engagement and well-being, and spurs not only creativity and collaboration but also analytical precision and productivity."

Stanford Graduate School of Business professor Jennifer Aaker and Lecturer Naomi Bagdonas coteach a course in business humor. They teach that "humor is an effective and underrated tool for power, offering a competitive advantage against peers, higher retention rates of employees, innovative solutions, and teams that are more resilient to stress."

Steve Tolak wrote an article in MoneyWatch titled "Why Leaders Need a Sense of Humor." He gave the following six reasons why he believed humor is the most underrated leadership trait:

- Humor is disarming—it puts people at ease. It relieves tension during crises—it helps employees to relax, think more clearly, and make better decisions.
- It softens the blow of bad news—it can let employees know we will win next time.
- Humor is great for team-building—when a team laughs and has fun together, it facilitates a sense of community and helps create a cohesive corporate culture.
- It gets people to root for you—your supporters will find you more likable, and your detractors will be more likely to cut you some slack.

- It places emphasis on key points—dramatic anecdotes, including the comedic kind, resonate with folks.
- Humor is motivating—a sense of humor helps keep people motivated, especially when times are hard.

Joel Stein, writing in *Stanford Business*, summed up the importance of humor very succinctly when he simply wrote, "Humor is serious business."

CHAPTER 7
LISTENING

Leaders and team builders must develop the skill of listening.

I directed a clinic in New York and went to dinner with John Wooden, sometimes referred to as the best coach in the history of American sport, and a high school coach. If you were a fly on the wall at that dinner and if you thought speaking was the key ingredient to intelligence, you would have thought the high school coach was John Wooden and Coach Wooden the high school coach. The high school coach did most of the talking and Coach Wooden most of the listening. The legendary UCLA coach had developed the skill of listening.

There was a study done of CEOs that I read years ago that asked them how they spent their time. The results were as follows:

10 percent—Writing
15 percent—Reading
30 percent—Speaking
45 percent—Listening

Almost half their time was spent listening.

My daughter, Colleen, is a lawyer in Chicago who negotiates many contracts. Because listening is a very important part of her work, she sees this quote every time she opens her computer: "I won't learn anything today by talking; but I will learn today by listening."

Will Rogers may have summed up listening best when he wrote, "Never pass up a good opportunity to just shut up."

Listening is a two-way street, and players have to listen to coaches, and coaches benefit greatly by listening to players. One year when we went into a game against Chicago State, a truly outstanding team with a great coach in Bob Hallberg, we had a 9-2 record. They were 10-1, so if we could win, we would tie for the conference title. The game and our season came down to two seconds remaining on the clock. At the time-out we set up an inbounds play under our basket. If *one* player did not listen to the play, our season is over. Our players did execute and scored to take the game into overtime. We eventually lost in double overtime, but there would have been no overtime if our players had not listened at that two-second time-out. Players must learn to listen intently in the athletic arena, and their eyes can play an important part in listening. I am sure I used an expression that I learned from Gordie Gillespie at that two-second time-out: "Give me your eyes." When I had their eyes, I hopefully had their brains!

Coaches can learn a great deal by listening to their team members. Our St. Francis volleyball coach, Rich Luenemann, produced national contenders annually. He convinced us that plyometrics would greatly improve our players' jumping ability, just as it did for his athletes. We made the decision to incorporate plyometrics at the very end of our practices. After doing this for a week, two of our senior captains and hardest workers, Shawn Schneider and Andre Thompson, came to us requesting that we stop the plyometrics. Their rationale was that we practiced very hard each afternoon and that the strenuous jumping drills at the end of practices might cause injuries. We listened and reached the conclusion that these drills would better serve our players in our preseason conditioning program. Andre and Shawn were total team players who wanted only what was best for our team—and we listened to them.

We had two delay games that we ran at the end of games when we were winning. It was not uncommon at a time-out for me to ask the players which of the two they wanted to run. They were playing the game, I trusted their decision-making, and I wanted them to finish the game in their comfort zone. Listening to our players and giving them ownership of some decisions enhanced our team-building.

Gordie Gillespie, as previously mentioned, was an extraordinary coach in all three major sports. His football teams at Joliet Catholic High School were 222-54-6; they won five state championships; and from 1975 to 1978, they were 51-1. His halftime talks were the Socratic method of teaching. They were composed of questions and answers. Gord would address a certain play, and the players would respond with how the opponent was defending it. From their response, Gordie would then make an adjustment in the play for the second half. He was such a respected football coach that when the *Chicago Tribune* picked the best players ever to play football in Illinois high schools—Dick Butkus, Red Grange, and so on—they picked Gordie to be their coach. And here was this legendary coach listening to fifteen- to eighteen-year-old players to make adjustments in games!

I once brought Rick Majerus into one of Gord's halftime sessions. When I asked him what he thought, his answer was, "It sure was different than the halftime talks I remember. All the coaches did was cuss at us and question our gender."

We have all kinds of classes in our colleges and universities in speaking. I have often wondered if we wouldn't better serve the students with classes in listening.

Listening is respect. When team builders listen to their team members, they are validating the respect they have for them.

From the Boardroom

Marry Barra, CEO of General Motors, writing in the Stanford School of Business, said this about listening: "It's okay to admit what you don't know. It's okay to ask for help. And it's more than okay to listen to the people you lead. In fact, it's essential."

She then went on to write, "It's important to surround yourself with people who will challenge you and tell you when and why you are wrong."

She finished by stating, "And the need to listen doesn't diminish when you become General Manager or CEO—it increases."

Peter Nulty wrote this in *Fortune* magazine: "Of all the skills of leadership, listening is the most valuable— and one of the least understood. Most captains of industry listen only sometimes, and they remain ordinary leaders. But a few, the great ones, never stop listening."

Betsy Sanders, former senior vice president and general manager of Nordstrom, had an interesting take on listening: "To learn through listening, practice it naively and actively. Naively means that you listen openly, ready to learn something, rather than to rebut. Listening actively means you acknowledge what you heard and act accordingly."

Lee Iacocca, former president and CEO of Chrysler Corporation, had this insight on true communication: "I only wish I could find an instructor who teaches people how to listen. Business people need to listen at least as much as they need to talk. Too many people fail to realize that real communication goes in both directions."

Bernard Baruch, an America financer, said, "Most of the successful people I've known are the ones who do more listening than talking."

It never hurts to heed the advice of people outside your work. In the first century, Publilius Syrus wrote, "Let a fool hold his tongue and he will pass for a sage." Oliver Wendell Holmes said it this way: "It is the province of knowledge to speak. And it is the privilege of wisdom to listen."

The Reverend Robert Schuller gave us something to consider when he wrote, "Big egos have little ears."

Frank Tyger continued with the ear analogy: "Be a good listener. Your ears will never get you in trouble."

CHAPTER 8
DISCIPLINE

Al McGuire said this about discipline: "When we win championships, we may cut the nets down with switch blades, but we are the most disciplined team in the country."

One of *Merriam-Webster*'s definitions of *discipline* is "Behavior that is judged by how well it follows a set of rules or orders." Al's teams certainly followed his orders. They played very hard at the defensive end of the floor, ran only on steals, and patiently ran their offense until they got a quality shot. They were disciplined.

Another definition of *discipline* states, "Discipline uses punishment to correct disobedience." This definition reminds me of a Rick Majerus practice. When a player made a physical or mental error in a scrimmage or a drill, he was immediately replaced and ran a sprint on the sidelines. The punishment was automatic and immediate. The athlete completed the sprint and got right back into the drill, but he had to wait for an opening to return to a scrimmage.

The origin of the word *discipline* comes from the Latin word *disciplina*, which means teaching and learning. How can there be learning if there is no discipline? It is needed in the classroom and the athletic arena, maybe more so in athletics. In the classroom, teachers teach, and students exhibit their learning when they take the exam. In the athletic arena, the athletes must first learn the coach's system. They must learn it well because when the exam, the game, comes, there is an opponent who is trying very hard to not allow the players—students—to execute the system they have learned. It would be like a student taking the teacher's exam with someone constantly trying to distract him by running a hand over his eyes during the entire time of the exam.

I distinctly remember a film session where we were teaching our players how we were going to defend an opponent's offense. As I was showing and explaining our defensive game plan, I noticed one of our players starting to fall asleep. I yelled at him that this was no history class, and he had better stay awake. The fact was, he should stay awake in history class to honor the teacher's work and to be able to do well on the next exam. The difference in athletics is that one player failing to execute our defensive plan would destroy our entire team's effectiveness. He did not have the right to let his teammates down.

There can be no success in athletics without discipline.

Today's coaches have a much more difficult time demanding discipline because of the change in parenting. When I played, if we were disciplined in the classroom or the athletic arena, the norm was that our parents automatically backed the teacher or the coach.

Bob Knight was asked how much kids changed during his forty-plus-year coaching tenure. His answer was the kids have not changed; the parents have. Unfortunately, too many kids are growing up with too little discipline. They don't hear the word *no* enough. When a psychologist was asked how soon should parents say no to their children, his answer was as soon as possible. His rationale was that saying no was healthy for the kids because life is a series of nos. I may want this car, this vacation, this house, but the answer simply is no because I cannot afford them.

Finally, the purpose of discipline is to lead to self-discipline. Remis Sasson wrote, "Self-discipline is one of the most important and useful skills everyone should possess. This skill is in every aspect of life. Self-discipline means self-control which is a sign of inner strength and control of yourself, your actions, and your reactions."

Through the years at St. Francis, we were very blessed. The great majority of our basketball players had self-discipline, and this was validated by the fact that 172 of the 176 seniors who played for us earned their degrees.

From the Boardroom

Matthew Keegan, in "The Importance of Discipline in an Organization," had the following to say on discipline in the business world: "The importance of discipline in an organization cannot be underestimated, since employee morale, productivity and even company profitability can be adversely affected."

Ruth Mahew, in "Purpose of Discipline in the Workplace," took discipline to another level when she wrote, "Disciplinary review and corrective action provide workplace structure. They establish guidelines for employee performance and behavior and add an essential component to the management system…Merely outlining workplace policies is not enough, management must consistently discipline employees who fail to adhere to them. This is the simplest way to enforce them."

Mary Strain, in "How Important Is Discipline to the Workplace," discussed ways of implementing discipline and the benefits of business discipline. She wrote, "Human Resource experts advise that workplace discipline is best administered in a private one-on-one conference that focuses on behavior, not personalities. And it's important not to ignore the issue. Workplace discipline, when properly administered, helps your business avoid many common problems and benefits you in many ways."

As in the athletic arena, the ultimate purpose of discipline is to lead to self-discipline. Adriana Girdler, in "Self-Discipline: The Common Trait of All Successful People," had this insight: "We all want to get someplace in life and in business. But why is it that only some people are able to get there? Is it because of luck, circumstance, or talent? Depending on the person it could be a combination of these things. The one common theme that does come up when conversing with successful people is discipline. Whether it's a business person growing an organization or an athlete wanting to medal in competition, discipline is the one element they all have in common. Discipline is the one fundamental element in obtaining goals, dreams, and desires."

Discipline, with or without Al McGuire's team's switchblades, does lead to achievement.

CHAPTER 9
TEACHER-COACH

When Hubie Brown spoke at clinics, he often asked the coaches, "Are you the best teacher in your building?" He followed that with "I don't care what you teach—biology, history, or math. Are you the best?" His point was that coaching is teaching, and if you fail to work on your teaching, you will never be a good coach.

Team builders have to be teachers. They have to teach their team members the philosophy of their organization and all the building blocks necessary to implement that philosophy. But teaching is only the first part of building the team. After the teaching is completed, the leaders must coach their teams to consistently give their best effort.

"I have not taught until you have learned." This is a maxim used in the teaching of coaching, and it should be the goal of every team builder in any endeavor. If team members have not learned, how can they possibly execute?

Great teachers do four things that lead to sustained execution:

First, they know their subject matter, be it an academic subject, a football team, or a business. As stated in the third chapter, they must not only know their subject matter, but they must be continuously learning it. We had a math professor at Lewis College—now Lewis University—who annually threw his notes away after teaching his classes. By doing so, he kept up with the changes in his discipline and his teaching methods.

Second, great teachers are organized. They can disseminate their knowledge. It is not enough to know your craft; you must be able to have your team members learn it. Some of us have experienced that brilliant professor who not only knows his subject matter but is an expert in his field. However, he cannot bring his knowledge to our level so we can learn. Even worse is the professor who spews his knowledge not caring if we learn. Teachers must be organized in their presentations, and the KISS theory (Keep It Simple, Stupid) does lead to learning.

Third, the outstanding team builder teaches with enthusiasm. He is enthused about his sport or his business, but he is most enthusiastic when he sees his team members learning and executing what they have been taught. Coach Jack Hermanski taught our post players. A friend, Scott Woltzen, ran a basketball camp for players to get the opportunity to play overseas. One of our players, Scott Pekol, attended the camp, and Jack and I went there for the final game. When we entered the gym, Tom Hehir, one of the visiting coaches from Ireland, introduced himself and told us Scott was the talk of the camp. He was outplaying the NCAA Division I players regularly. We watched the final game, and Scott totally outplayed a 6'11" Division I athlete. Jack could not have been prouder or more enthused as he watched Scott execute the post moves he had taught him.

Finally, great team builders and teachers believe in the first chapter of this book—they care. Team members know when their leader genuinely cares about their welfare beyond the field or court, and because of that caring, they go the extra mile for that leader.

Great team builders first teach, then coach their teams to excellence.

From the Boardroom

The following represents the importance of teaching in the business world.

Robyn D. Shulman wrote an article in *Forbes* titled "How This Teacher Left the Classroom and Built a 7-Figure Business." The article is about Jesse Jackson, who transitioned from teaching to business and shared this about the change: "I started my own business and am now using what I learned as a teacher and as a teacher-coach to help entrepreneurs create businesses that thrive, live their purpose, and make real change."

Timothy Sykes authored "4 Things Teaching Has Taught Me About Running a Business." His insight was:

I have created a successful business out of helping others learn about the stock market...I currently teach more than 5,000 students from 80 countries about the stock market and how to trade. Teaching has taught me a great deal not only about myself and about the stock market, but about business as well.

Here are four things that teaching has taught me about business:

1. Most people are lazy.
2. It pays to give and give and give.
3. Be open minded.
4. Utilize social media for every aspect of your business.

In "The Best Leaders Are Great Teachers," Sidney Finkelstein wrote the following: "Kamath Kundapur was a teacher. But he didn't work at a school or stand in front of a class. Instead, he delivered his lessons at the office—to employees who served under him during his four decades as a senior executive at, and then CEO of, India's ICICI Bank. ICICI became one of India's largest and most innovative banks, and Kamath has been credited with molding a whole generation of the country's banking executives."

Finkelstein went on to state, "The exceptional leaders I studied were teachers through and through. And it had an unmistakable impact: their teams and organizations were some of the highest-performing in their sectors."

The following represent the importance of coaching in the business world.

In "How Managers Can Become Effective Coaches of Employees," Dan McCarthy wrote, "It's quicker and simpler to give advice. Coaching takes a little more time and patience upfront, and it takes deliberate practice to get good at it. However, it is an investment in people that has a higher return than just about any other management skill I can think of. People learn, they develop, performance improves, people are more satisfied and engaged, and organizations are more successful."

William Craig wrote, "How to Lead Your Employees by Coaching" in *Forbes*. He stated, "Part of good leadership means seeing yourself as a coach, not as a king or queen who sits idly by and lifts the old finger to command. CEO's—it's time to lose the antiquated definition of a boss."

He then wrote, "Employees don't need a pat on the back once a year, nor do they need hand-holding every step of the way. Successful businesses achieve their goals through regular and effective feedback, communication, drive, and support. How is an employee to grow if a leader fails to coach the team? Encouraging employees in this way, will help you retain, empower, and grow your talented staff."

Kelly Pacatte authored "4 Ways to Coach your Employees to Success." She wrote,

Coaching and development are critical components of employee management and among the most worthwhile business investments you can make.

Here are some tips for efficiently coaching employees to their best performance:

1. Don't skimp on compliance, clarification, culture, and connection.
2. Lead like a coach, not a boss.
3. Give and receive frequent and consistent feedback.
4. Coach as a team.

Business leaders are teachers and coaches at their core!

CHAPTER 10
PLANNING

Planning is a strong component of team-building.
We had approximately sixty coaches in our athletic department at St. Francis, the majority of them off campus and part-time. As they were a big part of our team, it was important to communicate effectively with them. At the end of each year, our full-time people met for twenty hours—four hours per day for five days—and prepared our planning document for the upcoming year. The process was simple. We identified our priority items first, then all other items for the coming year. Our full-time people then wrote their goals in accordance with the planning document. We mailed the document to all our part-time coaches and set a date for a meeting with all coaches. At this meeting we went through the document, with each full-time coach speaking to his responsibility within the document. Through this planning, our part-time people had the opportunity to

read our planning document for the coming year and then listen to our full-time personnel speak to their respective areas. We began the year with everyone on the same page.

When our full-time people assembled to prepare for the next year, each of us read our goals to show what we had and had not accomplished. As the team leader, I always read mine first to let everyone know it was OK to fail to complete some goals. I don't believe I ever completed all my yearly goals, and I did not want our full-time people to feel bad about not finishing all their goals. I knew how hard they worked and all the sacrifices they made for our department and our athletes. Despite not completing all our goals, every year we did complete between 70 percent to 80 percent of our planning document.

We had the same quality of meticulous planning for our basketball program, with one exception that I highly recommend. Coach Jack owned a boat, and we held our planning meetings on his boat. Getting away from the office, with its many interruptions, was a blessing. Cell phones were also silenced. We would examine every aspect of our program and put our teaching in order. We also sponsored clinics in the fall for high school coaches. Each year we emphasized a different phase of the game—fundamentals, zone offense, special situations, and so on—and we wrote a booklet for the clinic coaches on the phase of the game we were presenting that year. This writing was organized on the boat, and we hoped the booklets would help the coaches. Many coaches told us they were very helpful, but they were especially good for us because they made us better teachers.

This planning made for a better athletic department and a better basketball program.

Finally, goals are certainly a big part of planning, and the most important facet of goal setting is that they be realistic. It was interesting how the goals of our basketball team evolved through the years. In our first years at St. Francis, only six of the twenty-one NAIA teams in Illinois made the playoffs, so our early goal was to be one of the six. Once that was accomplished, the goal changed to not only get to the playoffs, but to advance in them. Ultimately, it was realistic to set the goal of winning the playoffs and advancing to the national tournament.

Hubie Brown set an interesting goal when he took the Atlanta Hawks job. When he first saw their players, he immediately knew, given their talent level, they could not win in the NBA. He wanted to set a realistic goal, which turned out to be how many games could they *lose* by under ten points. If they could play the much more talented teams in the NBA to under ten, they would be showing the league that they were competitive. As the years passed, their goal changed to winning fifty games and advancing in the playoffs.

Meticulous planning combined with realistic goals can have team builders accomplish the five Ps—Proper Planning Prevents Poor Performance.

From the Boardroom
Rahab Messmer wrote "Four Reasons Why a Business Plan Is Important." He stated, "Excellent business ideas can be totally useless if you cannot formulate, execute, and implement a strategic plan to make your business idea work."

He then listed four reasons why you need a business plan:

1. To raise money for your business.
2. To make sound decisions.
3. To help you identify potential weaknesses.
4. To communicate your ideas with stakeholders.

Tim Berry wrote "How Business Planning Leads to Better Management" for *Entrepreneur.* He gave some interesting and disturbing opinions on business planning:

In my experience leading dozens of business planning workshops in countries all over the world, I'd say about only 10% to 15% of teams I've encountered have an effective business planning process. Sounds low, doesn't it? What many business owners fail to understand is that good planning equals good management. Here are three steps to get your planning better and, in turn, improve your management:

1. Devise a plan.
2. Define success.
3. Put it in motion.

He concluded, "Planning is management. Without planning, your management is at a real disadvantage."

Brian Hill, in "The Importance of Planning in an Organization," relates planning to team-building when he states, "Planning promotes team-building and a spirit of cooperation. When the plan is completed and communicated to members of the organization, everyone knows what their responsibilities are, and how other areas of the organization need their assistance and expertise in order to complete assigned tasks. They see how their work contributes to the success of the organization as a whole and can take pride in their contributions."

Benjamin Franklin summed up planning with a simple, pragmatic statement: "If you fail to plan, you are planning to fail."

CHAPTER 11
ATTENTION TO DETAIL

John Wooden said, "If you take care of the little things, the big things take care of themselves."

We had an outstanding president, Dr. Jack Orr, in our first nineteen years at St. Francis. He led the school from near bankruptcy to solvency during his tenure. After he retired I asked him, if he had to pick one thing that had led to his successful presidency, what would it be? He was a great listener, and I thought listening would be his response, but his answer was attention to detail.

Team builders have to pay attention to detail if they want to establish a successful organization.

The preeminent concept in our athletic recruiting was that we were recruiting for graduation. We most definitely wanted to produce winning teams, but never at the expense of failing to graduate our athletes. We used the following numbers to emphasize the importance of our players completing their degrees:

- 900 20 5
- 5,600 58 29 3½

The first set of numbers refers to baseball. The only longevity study I have ever seen on baseball tracked 900 players who signed out of high school. Because of their minor league system, baseball prefers to sign players out of high school as opposed to college. As they watched the progress of these 900 athletes, they found only 20 who made it to the major leagues, and only 5 played long enough to get a pension.

Each year there are approximately 5,600 seniors playing basketball in America's colleges and universities. We also have a number of players in colleges who fit the "one and done" category. The NBA draft has only two rounds, so 58 players get drafted. But when the smoke clears, only about 29 of these draftees make a team, and equally as important is that the average longevity of an NBA player is 3½ years. Recently I read that 25 percent of the NBA is now composed of non-American-born athletes, further reducing the opportunity to be drafted.

We shared these details with our athletes to let them know the chance of making a living as a professional athlete is truly minuscule. So there is no question but that athletes have to complete their degrees.

In coaching any sport, detail is very important. For example, in our basketball program, we taught all the fundamentals of dribbling, but there were two details that we emphasized that definitively led to dribbling proficiency—keep the ball low, preferably below your knees, and change pace. These two concepts, two little things, were stressed all year long. The same was true of passing the ball. We taught the fundamentals of each pass in the game, but we emphasized four details that led to passing proficiency: initially bring the ball down, only fake vertically, know the seven passing lanes, and pass away from the defense. Players who executed these four concepts became great passers.

When former DePaul coach Joe Meyer coached in the NBA Developmental League, he told me the players in that league really appreciated detail. Their goal was to make an NBA team, so any little detail that would make them a better player was worked on immediately.

Attention to detail is a must in becoming a great player and in creating a great team.

From the Boardroom
Ben Brearley, writing in Thoughtful Leader, stressed the importance of attention to detail:

Many managers and leaders are not detailed focused. That's fine. However, if you are one of these leaders, or plan to become one, then you better have somebody in your team that does care about attention to detail.

Spelling mistakes and grammatical errors are areas that people frequently raise as "nit picking" and "not important" to worry about. I disagree. Attention to detail can really matter.

As a manager or aspiring leader, you need to care about details. Why?

Because it's your reputation that's at stake. Do you want people to see you as a leader who doesn't care about doing things properly?... Attention to detail matters because if you don't care, why should other people?

Alex Cavoulacos wrote "3 Ways You're Not Paying Attention to Detail (and How to Fix It)." He had these insights into detail:

As a manager, my job is to enable my team members to do their best work, but also to serve as a final checkpoint for quality before that work makes it out to the world. As such, I've developed a few systems for spot-checking attention to detail, which makes me more or less confident in the work I'm reviewing. Pass the test, and the work gets my stamp of approval. Fail the test, and I'll be digging in to a lot more detail to make sure it's up to snuff.

I've listed out some of my quick spot-checks below so that you can catch those mistakes before your boss does—and keep impressing your colleagues with your unparalleled attention to detail.

1. Check for Accuracy
2. Check for Consistency
3. Check for Completion

Lisa McQuerrey listed seven points helpful in maintaining attention to detail in "How to Improve Attention to Detail at Work":

Overlooking details can sometimes be costly, detrimental to the quality of your work product, or in some cases, even dangerous. You can improve your overall attention to detail by using a few strategic planning and organizational techniques.

Create a Work Plan
Create a detailed work plan that outlines the individual elements in each of your key job functions.

Make Lists
If you have a number of things you need to accomplish in a particular time frame, make a list and check off each item as it's completed.

Plan in Advance
In addition to making daily lists, create long-term lists of projects that need your attention in the future.

Limit Distractions
Distractions limit your ability.

Maintain a Schedule
If you set aside a certain amount of time to devote to specific tasks, you're more likely to stay focused and finish the project with no interruptions or delays.

Avoid Overloading Yourself
When you add more work and pressure to a schedule that your brain can't fully comprehend and process, your productivity and effectiveness can decline.

Ask for Help
Employ trusted colleagues to look over your work and offer them the same courtesy.

Bob Boyd, the former University of Southern California basketball coach, used to say, "It's not what you teach; it's what you emphasize." And if you emphasize the little things, as Coach Wooden taught, the big things do take care of themselves.

CHAPTER 12
PRACTICES/TRAINING

We build athletic teams in our practices. I would assume other organizations and businesses build their teams in their training.

Dean Smith, the great University of North Carolina coach, used to say, "The practices belong to the coach; the games belong to the players."

Four thoughts on team-building through practices:

One of Vince Lombardi's favorite quotes was "Chase perfection and you might catch excellence." Coaches have to strive for perfection in practices, knowing they are never going to arrive at perfection but that excellence is most certainly acceptable. Lack of concentration, sloppiness, and poor execution are never tolerated because, as Gordie Gillespie often reiterated, "You play as you practice."

The second criterion for practices is that they must be physically and mentally demanding. When I have asked audiences in my attitude/leadership presentations to think of the best teacher or coach they ever had, I follow that with two questions, asking them to raise their hand on the one they agreed with. First, I ask, Was that teacher easy? No hands go up. Then I ask, Was your best teacher or coach demanding and tough? Inevitably, all the hands are raised. We learn in the classroom and in the athletic arena when we are pushed. Practices are where the athletes learn to compete and to compete hard!

We can also push ourselves in practices or training. When my son, Pat, finished college, he got the opportunity to go to work for IBM. His training lasted six months. His major was marketing, so he was behind many of his classmates who had majored in computer science. Knowing he was behind in the technology, he pushed himself. Classes went from 8:00 a.m. to 4:00 p.m., but he began his day at 6:00 a.m. to work on his computer skills. He pushed himself both physically and mentally, and his hard work paid off in the workplace.

The third criterion for practices is repetition. Coach Wooden believed that "repetition is the mother of learning." Don Shula, the outstanding Miami Dolphins coach, said it a different way. He believed the key to athletic teaching was "overlearning." Players have to repeat their skills so often that they actually overlearn their technique and their position responsibilities. Through repetition and overlearning, the following can happen in games. When action occurs, players:

- See Think React
- Read Relate React

Great teams and great players eliminate the middle word—they see and react or they read and react. They neither think nor relate because they have repeated the proper response so often in practices.

The fourth and final thought on practices is that they must be well organized. In my early years of coaching, I would organize the practices by the minute—that is, ten minutes on this drill, fifteen on the next drill, thirty on a scrimmage, and so on. There is nothing wrong with this, but I found myself becoming a slave to the clock and moving to the next phase even though we had performed the previous drill poorly. In my latter years, I simply wrote out the sequencing of the drills and scrimmages and watched the execution more closely, ending each drill sooner or adding time if necessary. We still accomplished all the practice agenda, but I watched the action more attentively.

There is an old maxim that the wise coach is like an owl—"The more he toots, the less he sees; the less he toots, the more he sees."

To build a great team, much thought has to go into practice or training sessions. Leaders must strive for perfection, be demanding, use repetition for lasting learning, be well organized, and observe intently.

From the Boardroom
Mike Kappel, writing in *Forbes*, examined five concepts that can lead to quality training in his "5 Tips for Successful Small Business Employee Training":

> Well trained employees are essential for any business. When employees have all the training, skills, and knowledge, your business will run more smoothly. Employees can perform their jobs with greater competency. They can better serve your customers. And, there will be fewer mistakes and accidents at your business.
>
> Use these tips below to create a training program and ensure the employees get the knowledge they need.

1. Create a Plan
Before you can make an employee training program, you must first determine what your employees need to learn. Otherwise, you might waste everyone's time with useless information and unstructured training.

2. Host Regular Training Sessions

You should regularly hold training sessions for your employees. Frequent training can maintain skills and knowledge.

3. Use Employees as Trainers

Even though you're the business owner, you might not know the nitty-gritty details of every employee's job. That's why highly skilled employees might be your best trainers.

4. Cross-Train Workers

You might teach employees to do other jobs within your business. Cross-training might help employees do their primary jobs better.

5. Set Training Goals

You must determine if your training goals are working. To do this, set goals and track whether they're being met.

Liz Ryan wrote "Ten Skills Every Manager Needs—But 90 Percent of Managers Lack":

Here are the skills that every leader needs but sadly most leaders don't possess. Traditional leadership training teaches people how to

Pat Sullivan

manage—but not how to lead, how to build trust, or how to be human with employees. It's time for a new approach.

Ten Skills Every Manager Needs

1. Every manager needs to be able to take in feedback from their employees—and not be defensive.
2. Every manager must develop the ability to take the employee's perspective and see things from the employee's point of view.
3. Every manager needs to understand how his or her function fits into the overall organization and how their business competes in the marketplace.
4. Every manager needs to learn self-reflection.
5. Every manager needs to know how to acknowledge and reinforce employees—and how to avoid bashing and criticizing them when they make a mistake.
6. Every manager needs to stand up for their teammates when a higher-up manager gives an order that isn't feasible or achievable.
7. Every manager needs to learn to manage his or her own career, completely apart from managing their department.
8. Every manager needs to learn to communicate with people of different ages, ethnic backgrounds, religions, political stripes, and personality types

and must learn to be open to a wide range of perspectives.

9. Every manager must learn how to build trust and community at work.
10. Finally, every manager must learn to be human at work, especially when conditions are ripe for fear-based management tactics to creep in.

Lisa Whealon centered on goals when she wrote "Create Training Programs Based on Your Companies Unique Needs":

> There are a lot of buzzwords thrown around in the training industry about how companies should execute their training programs. Sometimes we think we know what we should be offering our employees, but it's based on what's popular or what's trending.
>
> The goal of training is to provide our employees with education and tools that will help them and the business succeed. If you want to provide training that is valuable to you and your employees and the company, you need to tailor the training to what your organization and your employees need.

Training, like practices, leads to knowledge, discipline, and, ultimately, team success.

CHAPTER 13
WORK ETHIC

The leader or the team builder must be the hardest, most dedicated worker in the organization. If he or she is not, how can the team members be expected to give their all?

We always believed as coaches that the best teams were the ones where the best players were our best workers. If the best players gave the best effort, the rest of the team followed their lead. Dave Wilhelmi was an outstanding player for us. During his senior year, we actually rested him in some practices because he worked so hard and we wanted to save his legs for games. Dave played six years of minor league baseball before he came to us, and I am sure he developed his strong work ethic as a professional athlete.

Dick Butkus, one of the best linebackers in NFL history, if not the best, was the Chicago Bears' best player and leader. He led by example—he was the first player at practice and the last to leave.

The ultimate leader, the coach, must be a role model when it comes to work ethic. He must be diligent in his recruiting, his scouting, his film study, and his practice organization. When the athletes know the coach is doing all he can to put their team in a position to win, they will respond with their best effort.

Effort on the part of the leader is important, but of equal importance is that the effort be consistent. Many people can give great effort from Monday through Wednesday but cannot find that same effort Thursday through Saturday. The difference between a good team builder and a great team builder is consistency of effort.

Michael Jordan was the best basketball player I have ever seen. In his book *Rare Air*, he wrote that he learned something important about his NBA teammates when they all played together on the original Dream Team. Some of them simply did not practice hard. Experiencing this, he felt that at the crunch time of games, he would perform better than they would because of his consistent work ethic in practice.

Rumor has it that when a new player came to the Chicago Bulls, Jordan would really go after him in his very first practice, even to the point of embarrassing him. Some NBA teams and players do not practice hard due to the length of the season and all the travel.

Michael wanted to let the new player know that was not the case with the Bulls. If that new guy was going to be Michael's teammate, he had better equal Michael in his work habits.

John Wooden, as noted earlier, used to say "There are no shortcuts." When I think of the people whom I have met who have achieved in their respective professions, I can think of no one who did not work hard. Bishop Roger Kaffer was a great priest. Having worked with him for seven years at Providence Catholic High School, I know his work ethic had a profound effect on me and my fellow faculty and coaches. If our leader— he was at the time our principal—was committed to working so hard, how could we not follow suit? My good friend and former teammate, Ken Nelson, built a great furniture business. I saw how hard he worked and the incredible hours he put in to make his store the success it became. It was the same for Jim Gassensmith with his accounting firm. It became the success it became because he continuously studied his field and never stopped learning his profession. Vince Cornelius became president of the Illinois Bar Association because his peers knew how competent, bright, and hardworking he was. I could go on with numerous former athletes who excelled in their various professions, and I cannot think of one person who did not work hard to achieve excellence. There are no shortcuts.

Athletics is definitively an area where there are no shortcuts. You simply cannot get proficient at any athletic skill if you do not work at it.

Team builders ultimately are role models, and they must model a solid work ethic if they expect their team members to work hard.

From the Boardroom
Jacquelyn Smith wrote "The Insane Work Ethic of Mark Cuban, Jeff Bezos, and 14 Other Powerful Leaders" in *Inc.* and had this insight on work ethic:

> Talent, connections, and money can help you get where you want to get in life—but those things alone won't do it. You also need to work hard to be successful.
>
> Despite their obvious gifts, successful people like Kobe Bryant, Tom Cook, and Sherry Sandberg wouldn't be where they are today without having insane work ethics.

In Business 2 Community, Miranda Marquit wrote, "5 Traits That Prove Your Strong Work Ethic." She began by stating, "One of the most important traits of a good business leader is a strong work ethic. Your work ethic can help you build a good reputation in the business. When you make mistakes (and you will), your work ethic can go a long way toward helping others give you a second chance."

Marquit went on to list the five traits of a strong work ethic:

1. Professionalism: Treat customers, employees, and potential business partners with respect and dignity.
2. Dedication: If you are dedicated to achieving superior outcomes, it will show in the way your team performs and in the way your business succeeds.
3. Dependability: Dependability is a vital part of a strong work ethic. You need to show that you are trustworthy.
4. Accountability: Another way to show your strong work ethic is to be accountable for your actions. If something goes wrong you need to own up to your mistakes and try to fix them. Offering an apology when one is due is an important part of being accountable.
5. Gratitude: Show gratitude to those who help you. Show humility and gratitude for your success and give credit where credit is due.

Jacquelyn Whitmore's "7 Elements of a Strong Work Ethic," in *Entrepreneur*, is similar to Marquit's five traits:

A strong work ethic engages you and your employees to face your challenges head on, be your best and keep you at the top of your game.

Here are the seven key components of a rock-solid work ethic:

1. Professionalism
2. Respectfulness
3. Dependability
4. Dedication
5. Determination
6. Accountability
7. Humility

I especially like the three new elements—respectfulness, determination, and humility. All three advance and enhance a quality work ethic.

CHAPTER 14
COMPETITORS

One of the great values of athletics is that it teaches people how to compete. Don't we all have to compete in our professions? There are great numbers of doctors, lawyers, architects, accountants, and so on out there, and they all have to compete for business. Team builders have to teach their team members how to compete.

Competition is my second reason for not believing everybody should get a trophy. We have to teach young people how to compete. There are two main points of emphasis in competition. Competition necessitates hard work, and it should be done in the spirit of sportsmanship and ethics. Some people cheat to win. Unfortunately, cheating can sometimes work in the short run. But if you are in for the long haul, it usually fails.

Whatever your profession, you have to work to be successful.

In our basketball team-building, we strove to have our practices be harder than the games, especially in the defensive portion.

Like all defenses, transition was important to us. We divided the court into thirds—offensive third, defensive third, and the middle third. Games are often won or lost in the middle third of the court. Players tend to run hard in the middle third to the offensive end of the court because of the potential score. That reward is not available in running to the defensive end, but teams that compete do win the middle third defensive race. They make this transition because they know the adage that defense wins championships has merit.

Jack Ramsay, a great college and NBA coach, called defense "the great equalizer." The opponent may be better than we are, but we can equal their talent by making it tough for them to score. We therefore spent a great deal of time on scouting our opponents and on film work. We wanted our opponents to know from the very beginning of the game that we were prepared to defend them and that we were there to compete. If they were "to make a basket, they would have to earn a basket."

We also believed in Coach Knight's philosophy: "All of us can't be big, strong, or quick, but we all can be aggressive." To have our players see this in action, I would show them a segment of a game where there was a loose ball on the floor. Three of our players were on the floor getting after the ball, and only one opponent was in the picture. That was competing!

I would think in most professions, there are things people don't enjoy doing even though they know they are necessary for success. Players tend not to like defense, but without it there is no success.

It is not enough to compete with great work ethic; you must also compete fairly, within the rules of the game and the spirit of the rules. If you are cheating, what values are you teaching your players? What will they take from your program into medicine, law, business, or education?

We played against a team that had to forfeit all its games due to ineligible players. We played against teams that purposely kept the visiting locker room very hot to dissipate energy at halftime. We played against teams that were taught to hit the elbows of our shooters because the referees often failed to see it. We saw a team purposely, after a time-out, put the wrong shooter at the free throw line with seconds to go in the game. We played against a team where one of our players played high school basketball with one of their players. That player told our guy that at the pregame walkthrough, their coach told them, "Remember, take the charge tonight because I hired the officials." When the game was on the line, we were called for three charges in a row. An opposing coach once protested a game we had won, only to tell me privately that he knew he was wrong but his fans forced him to protest. We were not supposed to beat them, and their fans were very upset.

We definitely competed to win, but only with integrity.

Team builders have to get their teams to compete with all-out effort and to compete fairly.

From the Boardroom

Kaitlin Westbrook had this take on business competition in her "How Connecting with Competitors Is Actually Good for Business," when she wrote this in *Small Business*:

> Business Competition is the process of companies and individuals competing in the same industry or field. This sort of competition applies to virtually all businesses and employees.
>
> Healthy competition is good for business and more importantly, good for customers. Note what works for other businesses, then learn about your customers and apply that knowledge.

The next four writers believe there is good reason to hire former athletes.

Writing in *Forbes*, David K. Williams wrote, "Why You Fill Your Company with Athletes." He had this thoughtful analysis:

Athletes have the drive to practice a task rigorously, relentlessly, and even in the midst of failure until they succeed.

Athletes are tenacious—they seldom or never give up.

In his article in LinkedIn, "7 Reasons You Should Hire Former Athletes," Chris Vallette wrote the following:

They (athletes) are passionate about their work. They have been practicing and playing it for the majority of their lives, and they continue to play it with the zeal of day one...This is the drive that employers look for in potential employees.

Stephanie Vozza, in her article "Why Your Next Employee Should Be a Former Student Athlete" in *Fast Company*, quoted Vincent Mc Caffery, the CEO of game Theory Group as saying:

Businesses go through tough times and you can get kicked in the teeth. You want people to know that "no" is just one step closer to "yes."

To get to the college level, athletes have most likely failed more than they've won. But they always get up and keep going because they don't want to let down the team or the coach. In the workplace, this trait creates an employee who will find a way to win.

Finally, Jon Forknell, in *All Business*, wrote "The Benefits of Hiring Former Athletes." He had the following insight:

> It's hard to deny the competitive spirit of college athletes. They're in the game to win...Most have tasted loss and don't like its bitter flavor. These players fight hard not to repeat failure by working relentlessly toward their goal This same orientation toward goals is replicated in life after college. Athletes continue to be competitive by nature and want to do what it takes to reach the top.

We found in St. Francis athletics that many employers did look to interview our athletes for the reasons given above. It was not uncommon for an employer to call and tell us they were looking to hire an athlete, and could we recommend some for interviews? I believe they did this because they knew our athletes knew how to compete.

We then told our athletes if they were hired, they had a responsibility to future St. Francis athletes. If their competitive spirit made a difference for the company, the company would come back to St. Francis looking for future employees.

CHAPTER 15
CLEAR EXPECTATIONS

Team builders must let their team members know exactly what is expected of them.

I worked with a wise, older coach in my early years of teaching and coaching at Providence Catholic High School. His name was Bob McAlpin, and he had played football in the Chicago Catholic League and was a longtime coach in that famous league. As young coaches, we tended to have a lot of rules for our teams to follow. Bob was the first person to advise me to have fewer rules and to be sure to enforce the ones I had. As I continued in my coaching, I followed Bob's advice—few rules, clearly spelled out, and enforced.

Years later, I heard a college football coach say he had only one rule: "Don't lie to me." That became our number-one rule. If your players don't tell you the truth, you can't possibly work through the problems...

and there will be problems when you are in any leadership position!

One of our best players came to me and told me he had been caught with alcohol in the dorm. I first complimented him for being proactive and coming to me before I received a notice from the dorm supervisor. He did not lie, so we could work with the problem. He knew that we told all our athletes that we would never advocate for them when they failed to follow dorm rules. They were living in the dorm, and they had to follow the dorm rules with no interference from any coach. So that was the first order of business. Whatever punishment came from the dorm, he had to accept. Then we would deal with the basketball.

We expected all our athletes to follow all the rules of the university. One of my worst situations came over the Christmas break. We had both practices and games during the break, so our basketball team stayed on campus while all the other students were home on break. On this particular night, the only people in the dorm were our players. As I walked into my office to start the day, the maintenance staff came to me and said the players had been drinking the previous night and had the audacity to leave beer cans all over the dorm hallway. I immediately went to the dorm and could not believe the mess I saw in the hallway. I banged on each door, woke the whole lot of them up, made them clean the hallway while the maintenance staff watched, and then threw them out of the dorm for the remainder of the break. They still had to attend all the practices and get there however they could. Bottom line—they got what they deserved...and they knew it!

Our basketball rules were minimal, and along with them we gave our expectations, which were primarily academic. We expected our players to attend all their classes, be on time for class, and to let us know if they needed tutoring help in a class. We strove for exemplary behavior. We wanted them to show respect for the entire campus community. We simply let them know, why would anyone at the university come to see us play if we were not respectful on the campus? I wouldn't have.

It did not take our athletic teams very long to be successful because of Gordie Gillespie's leadership and the coaches he was able to bring to our teams. When our Chicagoland Collegiate Athletic Conference had been to ninety NAIA national championships, we had represented the conference in sixty of them. This was early in our program, and ironically, it had a negative effect with some faculty. The word spread around campus that all the coaches cared about was winning. We knew that definitely was not the case, so we did research that validated the academic success of our athletes. To market this success, we had a huge, professional sign made. It was the first thing everyone who entered our rec center saw. The very first thing on the top of the sign read,

"Academic Success of the St. Francis Student Athletes," and we listed the cumulative grade point average of our three hundred–plus athletes, the number of Academic All-Americans we had annually, and our athlete graduation rate of the seniors, which was 92 percent. Under the academic success of our athletes, we put "Athletic Success of the St. Francis Student Athletes," where we listed conference championships, national tournament appearances, and the number of All-Americans we had for the year. This sign let everyone know we were committed to academic and athletic excellence.

Team builders may consider few but enforced rules, integrity in all they do, and marketing their successes for everyone to see. These simple concepts led to clear expectations for our student athletes.

From the Boardroom

Susan M. Heathfield wrote, "Clear Team Performance Expectations" in The Balance Careers. The following was her insight into clear expectations: "A lack of clear performance expectations is cited by readers as a key contributing factor to their happiness or unhappiness at work. In fact, in a poll about what makes a bad boss—bad—the majority of the respondents said that their manager did not provide clear direction."

"The Best Managers—Always—Set Clear Expectations," according to Victor Lipman writing in Forbes: "Clarity is the pathway to solid results. As anyone whose worked in large organizations knows, clarity isn't always an attribute in abundant supply. With multiple players in multiple layers, it's easy to have communication and direction grow garbled...Clear expectations are a manager's best friend. Without them, clear results can prove elusive."

Writing in *Business News Daily*, Chad Brooks examined the positive and the negative effects of clear expectations in "Employee Success Depends on Clear Expectations from Leaders." He wrote, "Most workers are looking for a little more direction from their employers, new research shows. A study from Gallup discovered that half of all US employees don't know what's expected of them at work. Previous research has shown that when employees are focused on tasks that best suit their strengths...employee engagement and customer engagement increase, and turnover decreases."

Clear expectations in athletics and in the workplace are critical. They represent one of the cornerstones of execution.

CHAPTER 16
CREDIT

I f the team you build becomes successful, you, as the leader, probably will be given a great deal of credit and many accolades.

John Wooden and Gordie Gillespie were incredibly successful team builders and received much praise for their leadership. Although they met only once in their lives, they both held the same view on credit. Coach Wooden believed "Give all the credit away," and Gord constantly preached to coaches, "It's not about you."

Coach Wooden also taught me something that I always did in my postgame press interviews. The one thing we all see during a game is the player or players who are scoring. Naturally, when the reporters come to you after the game, they are going to bring up the names of the scorers. The scorers certainly deserve credit, but so do the guys who passed them the ball.

The scorers will get credit, so Coach Wooden taught us as coaches to address the players who made the assists and defended.

After winning a championship game one night at Providence Catholic High School, Roy King had a great game and scored twenty-six points. John Buchanan guarded the opponent's leading scorer who was averaging twenty-one points per game. He held him to one basket in five attempts, and he went one for two from the free-throw line. That player made only three points, eighteen points below his average, and we won the game by one point. I made sure John, whose work very well went unnoticed, received the credit he deserved. I knew Roy would receive all the credit he deserved.

I have great regard, as does every coach I know, for the DePaul University head women's basketball coach, Doug Bruno. Doug also assisted with the United States women's Olympic team for eight years. He has built a great program at DePaul.

I attended a big game for Doug for first place in the Big East Conference. DePaul against Marquette is a great rivalry, and both teams played exceptionally well that night, with DePaul winning in a great game. I was invited to Doug's postgame press conference. It was very inspiring to listen to him. He gave all the credit away. He thanked the crowd; the band; DePaul's marketing department for promoting the game; Jean Lenti Ponsetto, the athletic director; and naturally the players. Nothing was about Doug.

Having directed basketball clinics throughout the country for Medalist Sports Education for eight years, I met many coaches. Unfortunately, I met some who were the opposite of Doug. It was always about them and their great coaching expertise. They took all the credit. It was very difficult to deal with their arrogance. Thank God they were in the minority.

Bob Burg and John David Mann, coauthors of *The Go-Giver*, wrote this about leaders: "A true leader doesn't care who gets the credit. He just wants ideas to be received and his people to get the benefit." They could have been writing about John Wooden, Gordie Gillespie, or Doug Bruno.

Great team builders credit the people around them.

From the Boardroom

Ron Gibori had a great insight into giving the credit away in his article "The 1 Thing Great Leaders Don't Do" in *Inc.* when he wrote, "Leaders pass the credit and take the blame...They pull the thumb before they point the finger. Leaders recognize that an inspired team not only produces great work, but regularly strives beyond that extra mile to ensure success. Passing credit onto those under you is the best and the easiest way to do this. Why? A leader is nothing without their team."

In his article "It's All about Me! What Happens When a Leader Takes All the Credit," Joseph Folkman wrote, "The negative impact of taking credit for others' work is clear. However, the focus should be on the extraordinary value that comes from giving others all the credit. Many people underestimate the tremendous impact that comes from an effort to give credit to others."

John Boinott had this insight in his article in *Entrepreneur,* "Inspire Your Team by Living This One Leadership Principle from the US Marine": "The US Marines have 14 leadership principles. One of those 14 principles is unselfishness. To become a great leader, it is perhaps the single most important principle you must learn. This is true in the Marine Corps and it is true in business life. Servant Leadership requires that managers put their people first. They sacrifice to ensure that their people are in the best position to succeed and they unselfishly give to their people when things go well."

Snacknation summarized the concept of giving the credit away when it published "39 Thoughtful Employee Recognition and Appreciation Ideas for 2019," stating, "It pays to be really good at employee recognition. Companies with a solid strategy to recognize team members enjoy stronger engagement, increased employee morale, better customer service, and lowest turnover. Acknowledging achievement can have serious ROI to the tune of 50 percent higher productivity and as much as 20 percent increase in business outcomes."

Michael Jordan used to kid Jerry Krause, the general manager of the Chicago Bulls, that there may not be an "I" in team, but there is an "I" in WIN! But at the same time, he always credited his teammates.

CHAPTER 17
CRITIQUE

Action or person?

How a team builder critiques his team members is really important. When someone is not performing, he must be confronted. His poor performance is negatively affecting the team's performance, and it must be addressed.

I did address this issue in my first book, *Attitude— The Cornerstone of Leadership*. Those of you who read that book may be familiar with my thinking on this matter.

How can the leader critique his team members without hurting their confidence or their willingness to work?

In their outstanding book *The One Minute Manager*, Ken Blanchard and Spencer Johnson stress that the leader should critique the action, not the person. They believe by doing so, the leader is attacking the problem, the real issue. This allows the person being criticized to make the necessary changes while still retaining a positive attitude.

Many coaches in the athletic arena believe it is not enough to critique the action. If you want better performance, they believe you must also attack the person. I played for a coach who believed this. He constantly badgered your personhood, thinking this would motivate you to work harder. His criticism often had nothing to do with the action or how to correct your error. He simply wanted to put you down because he believed this would improve your performance. It was very difficult playing for him.

After this experience I played for Gordie Gillespie. When Gordie yelled at you or the team, you knew you had been yelled at! He could get quite angry and animated. However, in the four years I played for him, I never saw him attack the person. He strictly confronted the action.

Another facet of critiquing can be adding praise to the criticism. As previously mentioned, I don't believe there were too many coaches more demanding, more tough on his players than Vince Lombardi. Once again in his book *Instant Replay*, Jerry Kramer wrote that Lombardi could be very tough on you during practice. But after practice, it was not uncommon for him to put his arm around you and tell you that you were going to be one of the best players in the NFL. He would be rough on a player in practice but often praised him after practice.

Gordie could take praise to another level. He could praise you after you erred, when you were most vulnerable. During my sophomore year at Lewis, I relieved our starting pitcher in the seventh inning of a tie game. It was a tournament that we won almost every year. In the bottom of the ninth, we were still tied, and we had our best hitters coming up in the top of the tenth inning. I had gotten eight batters out in a row, only to have our opponent get three straight hits to beat us. I had let our team down big time. As I started off the mound, Gord was right there to greet me. This happened over fifty years ago, and I still remember what he said. "You walk off this mound with your head high. You will win more games for us than you will ever lose."

It was Morgan Wooten, the great DeMatha High School basketball coach, who first introduced me to the sandwich theory, where you sandwich the critique between two praising comments. For example, I could tell our point guard, "You know you are an outstanding player, so why would you make the difficult pass instead of reversing the ball and keep our offense running? Now go out there and show everyone why you are an all-conference player." I got my point across about not making a pass that easily could be deflected or intercepted but also didn't destroy his confidence.

Although I believe in confronting the action, not the person, there can be times when the person must be confronted. Whenever a player came out of a game, we wanted him to sit by an assistant coach so the coach could instruct him. We once had a player who refused to do this. Instead, he would go to the end of the bench when he came out of the game and pout. After being told our expectation a few times, he again went to the end of the bench in a subsequent game. At a time-out I had one of our assistant coaches walk him right across the floor and into our locker room. I told the coach to ask him one question when he got him to the locker room: Did he want to be a part of us or not? And I wanted an immediate yes or no as soon as I got to the locker room at halftime.

I did not care to embarrass our player right in front of the entire crowd, but he was embarrassing our team every time he came out of a game, and he had no right to do so. I was glad his answer was that he did want to continue to be with us, because he was a very good player who went on to have an excellent career—and he never went to the end of the bench again.

Team builders have to develop a philosophy of criticism. Criticism of the action, not the person, and praise may be a part of that philosophy until a team member deserves neither.

From the Boardroom
"How to Criticize Employees Nicely" was written by Amy Guettler, and she deals with softening the criticism:

> In a perfect world, managers would have no need to criticize employees. Everyone makes

mistakes, however, and every employee has room to improve. A productive employee does not require excessive supervision, otherwise, that employee wouldn't be on the payroll. When criticism is required, you can use a number of nonthreatening and constructive criticism techniques that inspire employees to improve their work, rather than make them feel inadequate.

1. During any critique, do it in person and in private to avoid embarrassing him in front of coworkers.
2. Ask questions aimed at uncovering any potential misunderstandings or miscommunications that may be the root of the problem.
3. Use the "sandwich critique" approach.
4. Focus on the issue, not the individual.
5. Clearly identify why the behavior is problematic, as well as what your expectations are for correcting the behavior.

Tip: If you're angry with something an employee has done, take a day to cool down before initiating a criticism. You'll be much calmer, have a better perspective and will be able to communicate nicely and respectfully.

Geoffrey James looks at criticism from a different perspective. He gives six thoughts on criticizing an employee who needs a "kick in the butt" in his article "How to Critique employees: 6 Rules."

Even if you're an experienced executive, it's likely you often find it very difficult to tell other people where they need to improve. Praising a good performance is easy; everyone likes to receive a compliment. But what do you do when a kick in the butt seems more appropriate than a pat on the back? Here's how to do this effectively:

1. Treat criticism as a form of feedback.
2. The term "criticism," while accurate, carries the baggage of negativity. By contrast, the term "feedback" implies the participation of both parties—a two way give and take where both people learn and grow.
3. Provide criticism on an ongoing basis.
4. Many bosses delay criticism until an employee's yearly performance review. That's ineffective, because the employee will be so concerned with money issues that he or she won't be able to concentrate on personal growth.
5. Dole out criticism in small doses.

If you stockpile problems, waiting for the "right moment" to bring them up, chances are the employee will simply be overwhelmed. Criticism is best given real time or immediately after the fact.

1. Begin by asking questions.

Your goal is not (or should not be) to persuade employees to do things the way that YOU would do them. Instead, dig deeper and find the roots of the specific problem.

2. Listen, acknowledge, and learn.

You may think you know what's going on and why something happened, but you might easily be wrong.

3. Address the behavior, not the person.

Never say something like "You're unreliable! You've been late three times this week!" Instead, address the behavior that's troubling, like so: "You're usually punctual, but this week you've been late three times. What's up?"

Diane Gottsman believes criticism can be inspirational in her "8 Ways to Use Criticism to Inspire Your Employees":

> There's an art to respectfully guiding employees with directness, honesty and dignity. When done the right way, criticism can actually strengthen the relationship you share with your staff and generate positive results. Here are eight steps for effectively delivering constructive criticism.

- Make communication a habit
- Focus on growth

- Balance criticism with positive reinforcement
- Be specific
- Avoid finger-pointing
- Be discreet
- Listen
- Follow up

Poor performance in athletics and business has to be addressed. I have found the longer you wait to address it, the worse it gets. The axiom "the sooner the better" is paramount here.

CHAPTER 18
BE YOU

Leaders and team builders have to be genuine. They cannot be phony.

There has been a change in our society that was referenced in Stephen Covey's book *The Seven Habits of Highly Effective People.* He wrote that success for the first 150 years of our country was based on character, integrity, and substance. However, as we progressed—or regressed—image came to the forefront. Image became more important than substance. Team builders without substance do not build lasting teams.

In athletics, coaches are constantly learning from other coaches. There is a continuous exchange of ideas at clinics and in coaching/teaching books and videos. We all learned from the great ones—John Wooden, Dean Smith, Bob Knight—but Al McGuire would always tell coaches you cannot be those guys. You have to be you.

When you are learning from others, you want to take the best they have to offer. We once had an NBA coach speaking at one of our camps who felt one of the campers was not listening to his lecture, so he threw a basketball at the boy's head. He wanted everyone in the camp to know how tough he was. The next day one of our young coaches was lecturing, felt a camper was not listening, and threw a ball at his head. He emulated the NBA coach, but he took the worst from him in his attempt to be like him. This was not the personality nor the character of this young coach, but he wanted to be like an NBA coach.

Team builders cannot be phonies, and we have certainly seen a number of phonies in recent years. Their image became more important than their substance. We've seen preachers promote Christian values but not live them. A number of our political leaders have created great images, but that was all it was—an image. Some coaches have promulgated all the positive values of athletics but have been cheating for years. Some business leaders have told their employees to keep investing in their company while they were simultaneously selling their stocks. These leaders may win in the short run but not in the long run, because their teams were built on false premises.

Clarence Darrow may have best characterized phonies when he wrote, "Some cause happiness wherever they go; others whenever they go." When the phonies leave, the teams can be rebuilt. They must go for the teams to last.

Don Shula, the outstanding NFL coach, often used a statement that leads to you being you and to team builders to being genuine: "Say what you mean and mean what you say."

No team builder can be a quality leader if he is trying to be someone else. He must have substance and be genuine.

From the Boardroom

I have always liked these quotes on being yourself.

"Be yourself; everyone else is taken." Oscar Wilde.

"Be who you are and say what you feel, because those who mind don't matter, and those who matter don't mind." Bernard M. Baruch.

"To be yourself in a world that is constantly trying to make you something else is the greatest accomplishment." Ralph Waldo Emerson.

"Don't compromise yourself—you're all you have." John Grisham.

"Always be the first-rate version of yourself and not a second-rate version of someone else." Judy Garland.

"Our time is limited so don't use it living someone else's life." Steve Jobs.

"Live as though nobody is watching, and express yourself as though everyone is listening." Nelson Mandela.

"You wouldn't worry so much about what others think of you if you realized how seldom they do." Eleanor Roosevelt.

"Be yourself; but always your better self." Karl Maeser.

"Just be yourself. Let people see the real, flawed, quirky, weird, beautiful, magical person that you are." Mandy Hale.

"Fearlessly be yourself." Anthony Rapp.

"The freedom to be yourself is a gift only you can give to yourself. But once you do, no one can take it away." Doe Zantamata.

Bruce Lee summed up being yourself with this quote:

"Always be yourself, express yourself, have faith in yourself; do not go out and look for a successful personality and duplicate it."

Oscar Wilde was right—you have to be yourself because everyone else is taken!

CHAPTER 19

TEAM EGO

Team builders should work to eliminate individual egos and build a team ego.

Jerry West was the best shooter I have ever seen. He played fourteen years in the NBA and played on one championship team. Oscar Robertson was one of the most complete players in NBA history. He too played fourteen NBA seasons and played on one championship team. However, Bill Russell played thirteen years in the NBA, and his Boston Celtics teams won eleven championships.

I have always believed you have to have talent to win, but talent alone won't win. It is only talent that is willing to play together that wins championships. Russell's teams knew they had talent and that their talent was committed to playing together. They validated that fact by making only two trades in the thirteen years Russell played there.

Russell said whenever the Celtics teams entered a gymnasium, they left their egos outside the door, but what they brought in was their team ego. They knew they were a great team and that they would bring a quality game every night. They did not fall into the overconfidence state, but they knew their opponent had better bring an exceptional game if they were to beat them because they were definitely going to.

When people think of Michael Jordan, they generally think of his scoring and that he was a great individual player. They seldom think of him as a great team player. Michael was the major factor in building the team ego of the six-time NBA championship Chicago Bulls teams. He was so much more than a scorer. He is the leading assist man in Bulls history. From my perspective, after watching him in forty or so playoff games in the Chicago Stadium and the United Center, he was not only the Bulls' best defensive player; he was the best defensive player in the entire NBA. He was also the most dedicated practice player on the team. Because the best player in the history of the NBA went so hard in practice, his teammates had no choice but to follow suit. Finally, his will to win was insatiable. His will was the ultimate driving force behind the Bulls' team ego.

Statistics can be used to develop team ego. We had one stretch over a two-year period when we outrebounded our opponents in sixty-four straight games. We shared this statistic with our players often, and it became a source of genuine team pride.

Our objective in every game was to hold our opponents at or under 40 percent shooting. When we accomplished this goal, we congratulated and complimented our players on a great team effort. We hardly ever mentioned individual statistics but always emphasized team statistics to further build our team ego.

Another facet of our team ego was the behavior of our players off the court. We wanted them to respect their fellow students, the professors, the maintenance staff, and all the people who worked on campus. For the most part, they did a great job of showing this respect. Whenever we received compliments on the behavior of a team member or the entire team, we immediately shared it with our players.

One area where we were especially proud of our team was their behavior in hotels when we were on the road. We often stressed that "our people" were not the owners of the hotels, but the people who cleaned the rooms. We wanted and expected those workers to be treated with absolute respect. We were very proud of our athletes when the hotel administrators told us they hoped we would return because of the respect our guys gave to all their employees.

Team ego off the floor was just as important as team ego on the floor.

From the Boardroom
Craig Bloem wrote "Want to Build a Great Culture? Start by Leaving Your Ego at the Door."

As the founder of a startup, it's not about you. It's about company—and your team's results.

An employee may disagree with you. An employee may say they would have done something differently. An employee may even talk down to you even though you're the CEO.

As a founder those moments are never fun. You have a choice. You can get defensive, snap back, or rest on your laurels as the founder.

Or you can take a step back, listen, think about what you hear, and create a culture where your team can share their feelings with you, even if their feelings hurt your feelings.

Accept criticism with grace, let the best ideas win (even if they aren't your ideas), and set an example for how other leaders in the company should act. If you do those things, your team will stay focused on results.

Julie Rains had these insights on team ego when she wrote "10 Ways to Help Let Go of Your Ego":

Open dialogue and collaboration can take your organization to the next level of success when exceptional ideas are embraced for their inherent value, regardless of the source. Being able to listen to grassroots and world-renowned thought leaders and champion employee engagement and customer-feedback require checking your ego at the door—and getting your managers to do the same.

Here are ways to check your ego at the door.

1. Focus on the team's goals, not individual bragging rights.
2. Recognize that creativity, wisdom and brilliance are packaged in many different forms.
3. Acknowledge that anyone can contribute to the conversation, analysis, and ultimately, execution.
4. Appreciate those who seem less astute than you.
5. Learn something new.
6. Solicit and apply useful feedback.
7. Be honest with yourself with your strengths and weaknesses.
8. Don't be afraid to try out a new idea.
9. After test runs, reflect on the worthiness of ideas and their execution.
10. Listen to people with whom you are supposed to be connecting.

Gulf Elite magazine featured this article that Bill Russell would appreciate: "Team First, Ego Last: Why Leaving Your Ego at the Door Is the Ultimate Mantra for Successful Startups." The author was not listed.

Having an amazing team is a crucial building block for any value-based organization, whether a well-established company with tens of thousands of people or a brand-new venture with a small nucleus of talent.

Best teams form when every person is committed to becoming his or her best self—starting with the founder whose personal values are the basis of the organization's values…Becoming your best self is an ongoing commitment to put the organization and its best team first—ahead of your own ego.

For those looking to establish a value-based focus into their company, here are a few tips:

Be Confident
True self-confidence allows you to recognize the uniqueness of your proposition so that you can sell it with confidence and authenticity to customers.

Act Humble
The value-based entrepreneur demonstrates "Servant Leadership," whereby the leader serves the team and together they devote themselves to the mission of the organization.

Focus on the Mission
On a value-based best team everyone, starting with the founder, is willing to subordinate his/

her ego. It isn't about any one individual. Rather, it's all about the team that serves the enterprise.

Communicate

Building a team of people who are aligned with the organization's values takes clear and consistent communication.

Delivering the innovative solutions and products to the marketplace takes a great idea. But the best way to turn that idea into a sustainable enterprise is by putting TEAM FIRST and EGO LAST.

Great teams in any venture build strong team egos.

CHAPTER 20
CULTURE

The hope of this book is that the previous nineteen chapters will lead to the culture you want to implement in your organization. Each concept plays an important role in building the culture. Once you have determined the culture you will implement, you are in a great position to recruit, find, or hire people who fit your culture.

When Gordie Gillespie and I came to St. Francis, our president, Dr. Jack Orr, told us the culture he wanted in the athletic department. He wanted three things:

1. Use athletics to increase enrollment.
2. Run the program with integrity.
3. Create an activity for every student.

Those were his instructions, and he followed them with "Winning will be a bonus."

We did accomplish the first goal, primarily because of the reputation Gordie had in the Chicago area. He had built a great athletic department at Lewis University, and his commitment to a comprehensive athletic program was widely known and admired. Every coach who came into our program, regardless of the sport, benefited greatly from Gord's sterling reputation.

When we arrived at St. Francis, there were only 45 athletes in three sports. At our zenith, we grew to 377 athletes in fourteen sports. Current athletic director Dave Laketa has done a superb job expanding the program to twenty-two sports, and there were 425 athletes participating in 2017. Virtually every athlete is on a partial scholarship, so the increase in the student enrollment has had a very positive impact on the university's financial position.

We did run the program with integrity. For a period of approximately seven years, we were a member of both the NAIA and the NCAA at the Division II level. We had to abide by the rules of both national organizations, and where rules diverged, we had to follow the stricter of the two. We never broke an NAIA or NCAA rule on purpose, but we did miss on some rules a few times. When we did, we immediately informed the ruling body, turning ourselves in. There was never a question concerning our integrity. We never purposely broke rules to gain a competitive advantage.

We created an activity for every student by implementing a very comprehensive intramural program. We had excellent student participation, and the students appreciated and enjoyed the activities.

Our president never varied from his "winning will be a bonus" stance. Never did he pressure us to win or ever even discuss it in the nineteen years we worked with him. However, because of the excellent coaches we were able to hire and the athletes they recruited, we did win. St. Francis has continued that winning tradition to this day and is a national contender in most sports within the NAIA.

The culture you intend to create should be clearly defined at the beginning of your endeavor, just as it was for Gordie and me.

From the Boardroom
"Maintaining an effective culture is so important that it, in fact, trumps strategy."

This was written by Howard Stevensen and shows how strongly he felt about the importance of culture.

Larry Alton wrote "Why Corporate Culture Is Becoming Even More Important" in *Forbes*. His insight was: "There is no single rubric for a 'correct' company culture—every business is different—but you will need a consistent and strong set of values if you want to remain competitive in the near future." Alton then went on to state some benefits of having "a strong, unified company culture underlying your business's operations":

- IDENTITY—Culture contributes to the identity and values of your company.
- RETENTION—A strong company culture attracts better talent and, more importantly, retains that talent.
- IMAGE—Corporate culture also adds to your brand identity.

William Craig, in *Forbes*, wrote "As Company Culture Improves, So Does Your Business." He had this to say about research: "Here is something that shouldn't be particularly surprising: After studying company culture as earnestly as any other business attribute, researchers have decided conclusively that culture is vitally important for the success of any company."

Writing in *Inc.*, Sujan Patel summed up why culture is so important in "The Importance of Building Culture in Your Organization": "Culture gives employees a driving goal and purpose for what they do. It connects your leadership team with the rest of the employees and binds them with a set of beliefs. Your employees want to feel like they are contributing to something bigger than themselves."

In the athletic arena and the business world, building a values-oriented culture leads to great decision-making. Decisions, in the last analysis, are based on your values.

CONCLUSION

1. **Caring**—"People don't care how much you know until they know how much you care."

2. **Knowledge**—Knowledge equals RESPECT.

3. **Continuous Learning**—Continuous learning equals WISDOM.

4. **Failure**—Developing a strong FQ leads to beating failure.

5. **Success**—"Success is never owned; it's only rented, and the rent is due every day."

6. **Humor**—Humor dissipates pressure.

7. **Listening**—"I never got in trouble with my ears."

8. **Discipline**—How can there be learning without discipline?

9. **Teacher-Coach**—Every leader is first a teacher, then a coach.

10. **Planning**—The five Ps—"Proper Planning Prevents Poor Performance."

11. **Attention to Detail**—"If you take care of the little things, the big things take care of themselves."

12. **Practice-Training**—"You play as you practice."

13. **Work Ethic**—The leader has to be the best worker.

14. **Competitors**—Everybody should not get a trophy. Everybody should learn to compete.

15. **Clear Expectations**—Have few rules and enforce the ones you have.

16. **Credit**—"Give all the credit away. It's not about you."

17. **Critique**—Action or person?

18. **Be You**—"Be yourself; everyone else is taken."

19. **Team Ego**—Leave your individual ego at the door.

20. **Culture**—Determine the culture you want to build at the beginning of your endeavor.

ABOUT THE AUTHOR

Author and speaker PatSullivan has been a successful basketball coach, teacher, and administratorin the Chicago area for over forty-four years. His high school and college teams have won 602 games. He has been named coach of the year eleven times and has been inducted into eight Halls of Fame. He has also received lifetime achievement awards from his alma mater, Lewis University; the Joliet Region Chamber of Commerce; and the Illinois Basketball Coaches Association.

Sullivan has spoken at the Chicago Nike Clinic and at US Coaching clinics throughout the country, and he's worked with businesses from Boston to San Francisco to improve team management. He's also shared his expertise at team-building camps and clinics in Greece, Belgium, Austria, and Ireland. His first book, ATTITUDE: The Cornerstone of Leadership, was published in 2013.

Pat has five children - Colleen, Katie, Pat, Anne, and Bridget - and thirteen grandchildren. He and his wife Peg live in Shorewood, Illinois.

SPEAKING ENGAGEMENTS

Pat Sullivan is based in the Chicago area, but he speaks throughout the United States and globally. He primarily speaks on two topics: the relationship of attitude to leadership from his book *Attitude: The Cornerstone of Leadership* and on team-building from *Team-Building: From the Bench to the Boardroom.*

If you would like Pat to speak to your organization, he can be reached at:

psully100@comcast.net

coachpatsullivan.com